Forever Faithful
A 21-Day Devotional

A Collaboration of Voices from
the Women of Grace

Copyright © 2025 Grace World Outreach Church

All rights reserved.

ISBN:9798319430199

DEDICATION

To every woman in every season of life. May you always know the Lord is forever faithful.

CONTENTS

Acknowledgments

1	I Once Was Lost	1
2	The Heart of Jesus	5
3	Abba, Father	9
4	A Perfect Father	13
5	Identity Crisis	17
6	He Who Promised is Faithful	21
7	Encountering the Great I Am	25
8	Make Your Petitions Known	29
9	Led By His Voice	33
10	The One I Can Trust	37
11	Reach Out and Touch Him	41
12	Is This Mine to Carry?	45
13	Freedom In Letting Go	49
14	He's In The Fire	53
15	More Than Enough	57
16	Woven By Grace	61
17	He Restores My Soul	65
18	Faith To Believe	69
19	The Anchor of My Soul	73
20	Living With Purpose	77
21	God Can Use Anyone	81

ACKNOWLEDGMENTS

To each woman who graciously lent her voice to this beautiful project, thank you. Your willingness to share your heart, your life, express how Jesus met you, carried you, and revealed Himself to you, is one of the greatest gifts you can give to others.

It is our prayer that as you read through these real-life experiences from authentic, Christ-honoring women, you will see Jesus in every word. May you feel His presence as you invite Him into each moment. And may you come to know, as each of us has, that the Lord is Forever Faithful.

I Once Was Lost
By: Victoria Jones

"For God so loved the world that he gave his only begotten Son, that whosoever believeth in him should not perish, but have eternal life." (John 3:16, NIV)

Since I was little, I loved beauty and perfection. From a young age, I felt restless to know the Creator of all perfection. No matter what I achieved or experienced, I never felt completely satisfied. I searched endlessly for something to fill my life.

In that search, I encountered many people and followed many different paths; New Age, astrology, astrological charts, but none of them brought me peace. They were all wrong way. I wandered through deserts and dry places, always thirsty, always longing for truth and the meaning of life. My soul was empty.

After much stumbling and heartbreak, Jesus sent someone into my life who showed me the right path. Gloria, my hairdresser for many years, spoke to me about the Lord every time I was there. One day she invited an evangelist to come to her place. She began reading Psalm 103 and I burst into tears. That was the moment.

God always knows whom He will use to bring light into our darkness. I received Jesus as my Savior, and everything changed. Just as darkness fades when the sun rises, the shadows in my life disappeared when

Jesus became my light and my priority. The things I once cared about lost their hold. He filled every empty space. I was overwhelmed by His peace and His love.

If you don't know Him, He is the answer to every question you have and the emptiness you feel. He is the Hand that lifts you out of the darkness. He is the way, the truth, and the life. He loves you with an everlasting love. Change begins when you invite Him to come into your heart. Confess your sins. Receive His forgiveness as you also forgive yourself and others. When you make this confession, you will feel the peace of His love wash over you. Your name will be written in the Book of Life when you declare Him as Savior and Lord. Allow Him to work in your life and draw you close to Him.

If you know Him but feel that you are in a dry place, the only thing you need to tell Him is that you want more of Him. He comes when we call upon His name. He will restore your joy. He will refresh you and make you new, and every dark place will be filled with His light.

Pray This With Me:

Lord, may Your love fill the empty places in my heart. Reveal Yourself to me as Savior and friend. Draw closer to me, restore my joy, and let me discover the abundant life You have promised. Let my soul never thirst again. In Jesus' name. Amen.

Reflection:

Are you searching for something to fill your soul? Take time today to talk with Jesus. Invite Him into every part of your life. Let Him be your Savior and the King of your heart.

_____
_____
_____
_____
_____
_____
_____
_____
_____
_____
_____
_____

The Heart of Jesus
By: Jerrica Ratcliffe

"I will give you a new heart and a new spirit I will put within you. And I will remove the heart of stone from your flesh and give you a heart of flesh." (Ezekiel 36:26, ESV)

"Lord, what moves your heart?" was my earnest prayer as I stood in worship one evening. I was desperate to know because it was that which I most longed to do. In His kindness, God began to share with me a revelation that has marked my life.

I saw Father God standing before me. I had just been the recipient of His Son's donor heart. I bore the scar from the transplant that had taken place. It was a reminder of the sacrifice that had been made for me. God approached me and placed His ear against my chest. Within me, He heard the sound of His Son's heart beating. "This is what moves me. Hearing my Son's heart beating in you." I stood in awe of the gift that I carried within me. Even still, I am captivated by that glorious thought.

As believers, we have been given a new heart. Ezekiel 36:26 says that God has given us a heart of flesh. Before salvation, we were dead in our sins (Ephesians 2), but now we are new creations in Christ (2 Corinthians 5:17).

Living in the fullness of this revelation means recognizing the power we walk in as bearers of Jesus' heart. It is an injustice to the sacrifice of Christ to return to the old mindsets and habits we walked in prior to our salvation. Would someone who waited years for a life-saving heart transplant ever ask for their diseased heart to be put back in? Of course not. The same should be true for us. We've been given the very heart of Jesus. Why would we ever want to go back to the life before we knew Jesus?

Let us live each day fully aware of this miraculous exchange. His heart beats within us. Let this truth shape our identity, our actions, and our compassion for others.

Pray This With Me:

Lord, help me to live a life aware of Your heart within me. Thank You that when I received salvation, You removed my heart of stone and replaced it with Your heart. Help me to move in rhythm with You. Keep my mind fixed on eternity. Help me to operate in Your compassion and see others through Your eyes. In Jesus' name. Amen.

Reflection:

Read Ephesians 2:1-10. In what ways have you felt your old habits and mindsets trying to take over again? What can you do today to walk fully in the new heart Christ has given you?

_____
_____
_____
_____
_____
_____
_____
_____
_____
_____
_____

Abba, Father
By Carissia Ratcliffe

"...for you have received the Spirit of adoption as sons, by whom we cry, "Abba! Father!" (Romans 8:15, ESV)

Friends of ours adopted 3 children who had only ever lived in an institution where they were malnourished, neglected, and abused. When my friend brought them into her house, even though they now had a home, parents who loved them, and plenty of food they still acted like orphans. They would tantrum as soon as they smelled food cooking or saw a meal being prepared because they didn't trust her to give some to them. When it was placed before them, they would hoard it or eat it as fast as they could. These children did not know how to receive or give love and were always ready to fight. It was heartbreaking. No matter what my friend said or did, it took years of trust to break those mentalities.

I couldn't help but compare those behaviors to my own son. He has never lived a day of his life without his needs and wants being met and trusts that I will always love and provide for him. He acts like a son.

An orphan is afraid of not being wanted, but God says, "For he chose us in him before the foundation of the world" (Ephesians 1:4). An orphan doesn't know their identity, but God says, " For we are his workmanship, created in Christ Jesus" (Ephesians 2:10).

An orphan fears being abandoned again, but God says, "The Lord your God is with you. He will never leave you or forsake you" (Deuteronomy 31:6).

If I'm honest I have spent a lot of time feeling like an orphan. Untrusting; unwilling to fully lean into my identity as a daughter out of fear. However, over the years I have learned to trust Him. He will not let me down or leave me to fend for myself. I am not an orphan. I don't need to live or act like one. I am a daughter. His daughter.

And so are you, my friend. You are not an orphan who operates from a place of fear or lack. You have been chosen by your Heavenly Father and received the spirit of adoption through Christ. You are deeply loved, and your identity is secure in Him.

Pray This With Me:

Abba Father, I come to You. Lean in close to my heart and whisper truth to me. Remind me that I am wanted, loved, and worthy because You say I am. I am Your daughter. You long for a relationship with me and for me to trust You. If I've been living like an orphan untrusting and afraid, speak identity into me. Remind me that I have been chosen by You. In Jesus' name. Amen.

Reflection:

In what areas of your life are you still holding onto an "orphan" mentality? Take a moment to list the areas you struggle to trust God in, and give Him full permission to be your Abba Father.

A Perfect Father
By Lori Othouse

"When my father and my mother forsake me, Then the Lord will take care of me." (Psalm 27:10, NKJV)

I stared at the screen, reading the words again and again. It was my father's obituary. His sudden death occurred only six weeks after my mom passed away, and I was struggling. Struggling with not only the fact that he was gone, but that I never knew him.

My parents never married, and by the time I was born, my father wanted nothing to do with my mother or myself. The only things I ever knew of him were stories from my mom, a few old photos, and a pitiful weekly child support check. I didn't know how to simultaneously process the grief of losing my mom who was always there, and my dad who was never there.

Looking back at the obituary, I noticed something. The listing of all the family members didn't include me. Not that I expected it to, but somehow seeing (or, rather, not seeing) it there in black and white seemed to scream to me, *"You never existed to him."*

The voices of bitterness, rejection, and shame, which I hadn't heard in a long time, began swirling in my head:

"Why wasn't I good enough?"

"Why did he never want to see me even once?"

"How could he forget us so easily?"

The voices ran pretty wild for a time, but then, slowly, above them all, came that sweet, familiar, still small voice, *"Don't forget about your real Father."*

Blinking back the tears, I could feel my heart and mind settle as He spoke.

"My child, I love you more than you can possibly fathom. I will always want you and I will never abandon you. I have given you My name and inscribed you on the palm of My hand. I gave My own Son to gain you as a daughter. My love for you will never change and is yours forever."

His love washed over me anew and, even though I was still grieving and struggling, I had my Father's hand to hold, and that was enough.

If you have been hurt, abused or rejected by a parent, know that you have a Heavenly Father who loves you perfectly. His love is not conditional, unstable, or confusing. It is constant and true because He is love. Whatever we lack in human relationships, He is more than able to make up for in our relationship with Him. Run to Him, let Him hold you close, and feel the kind of love only the Father can give.

Pray This With Me:

Lord, help me to remember that You are my Heavenly Father not in name only, but in relationship. Guard my heart and mind against the voices of shame and rejection. Help me to always remember who I am in You, a daughter who is perfectly loved. In Jesus' name. Amen.

Reflection:

How can you draw closer to God as your Father? In what areas can you trust Him more, knowing His love for you is perfect?

_____
_____
_____
_____
_____
_____
_____
_____
_____
_____
_____

Identity Crisis
By: Anne-Marie Gallimore

"And He (Jesus) asked them, 'But who do you yourselves say that I am?' Peter replied to Him, 'You are the Christ (the Messiah, the Anointed One).'" (Mark 8:29, AMPC)

When someone asks, *"Who are you?"* We often respond with titles or roles: "I'm a nurse, a mom, a friend, a student." But those are *what* we do—not *who* we truly are.

In order for us to rightly see ourselves, we first need to rightly see Jesus. This helps us know our identity. If you've accepted Jesus Christ as your personal Lord and Savior, your identity has shifted. You are no longer defined by your past, your job, or your social status. You are now a child of God. You've moved from darkness into light. You are the righteousness of God in Christ (2 Corinthians 5:21).

Jesus knew who He was. His confidence came from His Father's affirmation: *"You are My Beloved Son, in You I am well pleased"* (Mark 1:11, AMPC.) In the same way, your identity has been affirmed by God—not based on your performance, but on who He says you are, His daughter.

Your righteousness is a gift from God. It doesn't vanish when you mess up. That angry word, that mistake, that doubt does not take from you what Jesus gave you. Righteousness was placed on you like a cloak the moment you said yes to Jesus.

Life throws heavy things our way: a diagnosis, a job loss, grief, or financial strain. But when we know who we are, we don't cower, we fight. Not with fists, but with the Word of God, which is "sharper than any two-edged sword" (Hebrews 4:12, AMPC).

Speak His promises daily. Remind your soul:

"I am righteous."

"I am chosen."

"I am deeply loved by God."

I had to learn this truth when, many years ago, I became pregnant after a miscarriage the year before. The thoughts began to overwhelm me: "Will I miscarry again at twenty-two weeks? Will this baby survive? Am I a failure as a woman? Why couldn't I preserve the last pregnancy?" I had to read and repeat God's Word, *"I am the righteousness of God in Christ, I am loved by God and He gives good gifts to me,"* many times until it settled my heart and mind and peace came.

Pray This With Me:

Take a moment today to look in the mirror and say this prayer: Father, thank You for making me righteous through Jesus's sacrifice on the Cross. Thank You that I'm your daughter, loved by You, chosen, and called to show others Your goodness. Remind me to speak truth over myself to help me remember who I am. In Jesus' name. Amen.

Reflection:

When asked who you are, how do you respond? Is your answer rooted in what the world says or what God says? Where have you let circumstances or past pain shape your identity more than the truth of God's Word? What truth do you need to speak over yourself today to stand firm in who He says you are?

He Who Promised Is Faithful
By: Jenna Norris

"...He who promised is faithful." (Hebrews 10:23, NKJV)

Each year, I follow a reading plan to read through the Bible in a year and came across a familiar story, God's promise to Abram that he would be the father of many nations. I've read these verses many times, but this time, realizing that this was a big promise that both Abram and Sarai were waiting on, yet had no son to see this promise fulfilled. I began to wonder what their late-night conversations were like. Did they go back and forth between hope and doubt? Did they wonder if they really heard God?

If we're honest, many of us have been there. Waiting is hard. Patience is hard. When promises don't come to pass the way or when we expect, our hearts grow weary.

Maybe you've felt disappointed that something hasn't happened the way you thought it would. Perhaps you've felt lonely like no one understands what you're going through. It's possible you have played the comparison mind game and everyone else is seeing their promise fulfilled except you. Or even doubting that you heard God clearly.

I imagine that is the way Sarai felt.

In our desperation, we sometimes take matters into our own hands. Sarai knew God's promise, but because she couldn't see it unfolding. S chose to act in the flesh. The result was a son not born of promise but of human striving. It's a reminder to us: not to fulfill God's promises through our own means.

Let me challenge you to move from disappointment to hope. God is still writing your story. He will finish what He started. Instead of feeling lonely, draw near to God. You are never alone. God is with you in the waiting. Choose to believe, have faith, and do not doubt. Be content and celebrate others as you trust God. Keep your eyes on the One who is faithful to His Word.

I've been there before, too. Our family was in a season of waiting and holding on to what the Lord had said. I wrote this in my journal: *"Remain steadfast in waiting for the promise. Do not waver. Do not try to figure it out. Do not settle for a "Hagar solution." Hold fast to His Word. He does not lie. Trust Him. Seek Him. He rewards those who diligently seek Him. Delay does not mean denial."*

When we lose sight of the promise, we often stop speaking and believing it. That's why it's important to keep our eyes and heart focused on what God has said because He who promised *is* faithful.

Pray This With Me:

Lord, help me to wait. Teach me to trust You even when I don't understand the timing or the way. Guard my heart from trying to make it happen in my own strength. Keep my eyes fixed on Your promises. Remind me that You are always faithful. In Jesus' name. Amen.

Reflection:

What promise are you holding onto right now, and how can you strengthen your trust in God's perfect timing?

_____
_____
_____
_____
_____
_____
_____
_____
_____
_____
_____
_____

Encountering The Great I Am
By: Analysa Fullam

"So Moses thought, 'I must go over and look at this remarkable sight. Why isn't the bush burning up?' When the Lord saw that he had gone over to look, God called out to him from the bush, 'Moses, Moses!' 'Here I am,' he answered. 'Do not come closer,' he said. 'Remove the sandals from your feet, for the place where you are standing is holy ground.'" (Exodus 3:3-5, CSB)

As women, we often find ourselves living off experiences rather than truly encountering God. Let's face it. We are all busy. I can't remember what dry shampoo day I'm on, and my boys have been eating frozen chicken nuggets for days now because I haven't been grocery shopping. I get it.

We hear powerful testimonies, read devotionals, and listen to messages that inspire us, but do we truly make the time to encounter The Great I Am?

You see, an experience focuses on what you feel or receive. An encounter focuses on what God is doing in you, leading to lasting change. Moses could have stayed at a distance, simply observing the burning bush. He would have had a great story to tell, but instead, he moved closer. That's when God spoke, "Moses, remove your sandals, for the ground you are standing on is holy ground."

Our *sandals* represent things we carry; our past, our burdens, unholy/unclean things, areas of compromise, and distractions. We often think our sin isn't as bad as someone else's or isn't a big deal. But to get closer to the fire, we must be willing to remove the unclean things from our lives. In other words, take off our "sandals".

Often, we prefer to stand at a distance, content on experiencing His presence, because we know getting closer requires surrender.

For some of us, surrender looks like letting go of comparison measuring our worth against other moms or women. It means releasing control and trusting God with our families, marriages, and futures instead of holding everything tightly. It means forgiving and letting go of bitterness and resentment and trusting God with our wounded hearts. It means silencing distractions like social media, busyness, and the noise that drowns out His voice.

We can't live off secondhand faith. A relationship with God cannot be built on borrowed experiences. It's meant to be personal and deep.

You don't get the deep things of God by going to the drive-thru lane of His presence. If you want true encounters with His voice and His presence, you have to be willing to stay awhile…consistently.

God is calling us to draw near. But getting closer requires surrender. It requires us to trust Him enough to let go. The question is: Are we willing to take off our sandals and stay for a while?

Pray This With Me:

Lord, I don't want to settle for temporary experiences with You. I want a true encounter. Show me what I need to surrender so that I can step into Your presence fully. Help me to remove anything that is keeping me from You. In Jesus' name. Amen.

Reflection

What "sandals" do you need to remove to experience a real encounter with God? Pray about what God is asking you to surrender. Make space for Him to speak. Stop living off experiences and start encountering The Great I Am.

Make Your Petitions Known
By Cindy Lewis

"...and the Lord has granted me my petition that I made to Him." (Samuel 1:27, NKJV)

Crises happen to all of us. Desperate times come, and in those moments, we are faced with a choice: run from God or run to Him.

On May 20, 2018, my husband and I began a journey that would forever change us. Early that morning, I was awakened by my husband saying, "Cindy, I cannot get up." We went to the hospital, and I watched paralysis race up his body in the ICU. Doctors warned it might continue.

In the middle of this desperate moment, this scripture overwhelmed my thoughts, my heart, and my soul. It became my anchor. I began calling every church and every prayer chain I could think of to petition God together—not just for healing, but specifically that the paralysis would not reach his voice. His voice is his ministry, his calling. I was desperate to see God move, and He did. God heard, and He answered.

This scripture is about a woman named Hannah who was desperate for a son. She was ridiculed because she was barren. Even the priest mistook her for a drunk. She couldn't even speak because of the weight of her desperation. Hannah ran to God face-down in surrender and made her request known. God answered and gave her a son, Samuel, which means "God has heard."

Hannah's story and mine are both stories of deep desperation, faithful prayer, ultimate surrender, and unwavering trust. Though painful, choosing to never turn away from God, but choosing to run *to* God.

Here's what I learned and what I hope you learn when facing a difficult situation: you can completely surrender to God. You're never alone or without hope no matter how hopeless it may seem. We all face challenges, but God promises that He will never leave us or forsake us.

In that season, I was broken and desperate for God to hear. In that brokenness, I received strength, encouragement, and a deeper more intimate relationship with Him. I ran to Jesus and held on to His Word because His Word is truth.

This journey has taught me surrender, brokenness, faith, confidence, and a deeper love for my husband and my God. It showed me the importance of having an inner circle of friends who love God, who will be there for you, and you for them, no matter the situation.

Pray This With Me:

Father God, at every turn in my life, let me always look to You, knowing that You are for me and not against me. You see all things and are there during every storm. Lord, I trust You and surrender everything to You. In Jesus' name. Amen.

Reflection:

Are you facing a situation right now that feels desperate or overwhelming? I encourage you to find a "go-to Bible verse" that speaks to you personally and encourages your heart. Run to Jesus and know that He hears your every prayer.

_____
_____
_____
_____
_____
_____
_____
_____
_____
_____

Led By His Voice
By: Jeverna King

"Your own ears will hear him. Right behind you a voice will say, "This is the way you should go," whether to the right or to the left." (Isaiah 30:21, NLT)

I love to travel, especially to new places I've never been before. But if I'm traveling by car, I usually need the help of a navigation app to get me to that new place.

Recently, my family and I were on a new adventure, and I was helping with directions. We followed every turn and back road that the voice on the navigation app directed us to. But when we arrived, it turned out not to be the right place after all.

I began to panic and even cried in frustration because I thought we were at the right place. I had no clue what went wrong. After several hours on the road, we were exhausted, our boys were exhausted and all we wanted to do was reach our Airbnb for the night.

After collecting my thoughts and receiving much needed assurance from my husband, I realized I had typed in the wrong word in part of the address. I re-entered the correct address, and we finally made it to the right location and celebrated with much relief, excitement, and even a few laughs at ourselves.

I often see how life's circumstances relate to my relationship with God. Just like a GPS gives us directions, God leads us in the plans and purposes He has for us—even when there are detours or unexpected stops along the way. In those moments, we remember that God has good plans, a purpose, and even unexpected joys to experience!

But sometimes, along the journey of following God and doing what He's asked us to do, we can feel unsure about the unknown. There can be moments of frustration, doubt, and fear—questioning if we are in the right place, doubting if we are hearing God's voice, and feeling overwhelmed by change.

Isaiah 30:21 says, "Your own ears will hear him. Right behind you, a voice will say, 'This is the way you should go,' whether to the right or to the left." God still speaks today, and He is faithful to lead us when we listen for His voice and trust Him.

God speaks in various ways whether through Scripture, creation, impressions, circumstances, and even other people. When He speaks, it's to guide, comfort, help, strengthen, correct, and empower and ultimately, to reveal His love to us and through us! He loves us so much that He will take the wrong turns of our lives; the challenges, the obstacles, the crooked places and make our paths straight. He will show us the way we should go.

Pray This With Me:

God, thank You for speaking to me and for leading me. I surrender my life to You and choose to trust You when fear, doubt, or the unknown want to overwhelm me. Make me sensitive to Your voice and help me to recognize where You're leading me. In Jesus' name, Amen.

Reflection:

Describe a time when you sensed God leading you to step into something new. What is God speaking to you now?

_____
_____
_____
_____
_____
_____
_____
_____
_____
_____
_____
_____

The One I Can Trust
By: Jenna Norris

"Trust in the Lord with all your heart and lean not on your own understanding." (Proverbs 3:5, NIV)

Do you ever find it hard to trust God?

It's easy to encourage others when they're walking through something difficult. We say, "Surrender it all to Jesus. You can trust Him," and we mean it. But when the situation becomes personal and you're the one facing the unexpected, it often becomes difficult. In these moments, it is important that our behavior aligns with what we believe.

So why is it that when it comes to trusting God, we sometimes hesitate?

There is no reason not to wholeheartedly trust Him. He's never failed. He never will. It's not even in His nature to fail. He's good. He's faithful. He always has our best in mind.

I know that. I *believe* that.

But in teh moments when life happens, when something unexpected takes place or the future feels uncertain, I tend to overthink. I begin to wonder how it is all going to work out. I get nervous. Guarded. Unwilling to surrender it all to the very One I *know* I can trust the most.

In Luke 7, we are introduced to a woman who came into a room where Jesus was, uninvited, she broke open an alabaster jar and poured out the costly perfume onto His feet. It was an extravagant moment of worship.

Those who were in the room knew her story. Decisions she had made led to a life and people that had been unkind to her. She was unaware of where to go and who to trust. Until she met Jesus and her response was to give Him everything, no matter what it cost.

To everyone else this was foolish, but to Jesus this was priceless. She was priceless.

It wasn't an emotional response, it was complete and total surrender. Trust. Her past was one of trusting her heart to the wrong people, but in that moment, she chose Jesus to hold it all. He did not break her heart or let her down.

That's the kind of trust we need to have.

When we are overwhelmed and unsure of where to place our trust, we can come to Jesus, bringing everything to His feet in worship and surrender. Our response needs to line up with what we truly believe... that we can trust Jesus with everything. He sees. He knows. He's not afraid of your story. In fact, He is still writing it.

Pray This With Me:

Jesus, You are the One I can trust. When I feel uncertain, overwhelmed, or afraid, remind me that You've never failed and You never will. Help me bring every part of my heart to You, the broken pieces, and fears I try to hide. Let me lay it all at Your feet. Teach me to trust You more and to worship You with everything I have, no matter the cost. In Jesus' name. Amen.

Reflection:

What part of your heart are you holding back from Jesus? Where is He inviting you to trust Him? Take a moment to bring it to His feet and allow what you believe to shape the way you respond.

_____
_____
_____
_____
_____
_____
_____
_____
_____
_____
_____
_____

Reach Out and Touch Him
By: Debbie Milton

"Daughter, your faith has made you well. Go in peace and be healed of your affliction." (Mark 5:34, ESV)

When my youngest daughter was just four years old, she was diagnosed with a chronic kidney disease that severely weakened her immune system. For years, she battled frequent illnesses, ear infections, sinus issues, and bacterial and viral infections. Her childhood was marked not only by missed school and hospital visits but also by a quiet resilience. She rarely complained, even when her body was weary. She pressed on through every season of sickness.

At age sixteen, she reached her breaking point during a Friday night football game. She had just finished the halftime performance as a band member and came to us in tears. "Mom, I'm just tired of being sick all the time," she cried. Her words pierced my heart.

We were sitting with our new pastors, and my husband began to explain her struggles to them. He said, "Maybe God hasn't healed her because He knows it keeps us on our knees." Our pastor's wife, with eyes full of determination, pointed her finger at us and declared, "My God does not keep people sick so their parents will pray. My God is a healer."

Her words were a wake-up call. She challenged us to search the Scriptures for what God's Word says about healing. Mark 5:34 became our anchor: "Daughter, your faith has made you well." Like the woman with the issue of blood who pressed through the crowd to touch Jesus' robe, we reached out in faith, daily and deliberately. I found a new healing scripture each day and posted it on our refrigerator. She read it. We said it together. We believed. Over time, our faith grew strong.

Three years later, at age nineteen, she went in for routine blood work. Her doctor called with bewildering news: "I don't understand it. Her blood shows no signs of the disease. This type doesn't go into remission. I've never seen anything like it." But we knew exactly what had happened.

God had healed our daughter—not instantly, but undeniably. Faith had reached out and touched Him. And He responded.

Friend, maybe today you're like that woman in Mark 5. You've carried an affliction, a pain, or a burden for far too long, but Jesus is still passing by. He is still the Healer. Faith is not wishful thinking. It is standing firm on the Word of God and believing that what He said, He will do.

Pray This With Me:

Lord Jesus, I believe. Help my unbelief. Stir up my faith as I read Your Word and stand on Your promises. You are my Healer, Yahweh Rapha is Your name. I reach out to You today, trusting in Your mercy and power. In Jesus' name. Amen.

Reflection:

Today, begin your own journey of faith. Find a scripture about healing and speak it aloud. Write it down. Post it where you'll see it daily. Let faith arise as you hear God's Word and believe that Jesus still heals - spirit, soul, and body. Reach out and touch Him.

Is This Mine To Carry?
By: Charlotte Edwards

"Come to me, all you who are weary and burdened, and I will give you rest... For my yoke is easy and my burden is light."
(Matthew 11:28-30, NIV)

It started with a conversation with our adult daughter. She had asked us to help her with something, and I'll be honest, I didn't want to commit. In my mind, I was thinking, *"Tell her this isn't our problem."* However, before I spoke, I sensed the Lord nudging my heart, not to focus on whether it was my problem, but to gently tell her, "This is your responsibility."

That simple shift changed something in me. I began to reflect on how often I had picked up things that weren't mine to carry always trying to fix, manage, or control situations that God never assigned to me. And I started asking myself, *"How many responsibilities have I taken on that were never mine to begin with?" Are there things I have said yes to even when I didn't want to say yes, simply because I felt that I would disappoint the other person?"*

Jesus invites us to come to Him when we're weary and burdened. He offers rest, not by removing all responsibilities, but by helping us discern which ones are truly ours to carry, and giving us strength and peace for those He's entrusted to us.

Maybe, like me, you've found yourself carrying the emotional weight of issues that aren't yours to fix. Taking on tasks you weren't called to, just to keep the peace. Experiencing anxiety about things only God can control or even guilt that pushes you into "yes," even when your spirit says "no".

Let me encourage you to pause and ask: *"Is this mine to carry?"* When we begin to sort through what's ours and what's not, we make space to live lighter and walk more freely.

We shift from:

Overwhelmed to Focused: When we identify what truly belongs to us, clarity replaces chaos, and we can move forward with purpose.

Guilt to Grace: Releasing what's not ours brings us personal peace.

Control to Trust: Releasing our grip allows room for God to move, reminding us that He's more than capable.

Busyness to Purpose: By carrying only what's meant for us, we create margin for joy.

Surrendering unnecessary responsibility isn't selfish—it's faithful stewardship. It frees us up to show up better, love others wisely, and live in the grace God has given us.

Pray This With Me:

Lord, show me what You've called me to carry and give me the wisdom to lay down what is not mine. I want to walk in step with You, trusting Your grace for what's mine, and releasing everything else into Your care. Thank You for being my strength and my peace. In Jesus' name. Amen.

Reflection:

What burden have you been carrying that may not be yours to carry? Take a moment to ask the Lord to show you what you need to release and trust Him to carry what only He can.

The Freedom In Letting Go
By: Kier Rodas

"In their hearts humans plan their course, but the Lord establishes their steps."(Proverbs 16:9, NIV)

I've always been a planner. As an A-type personality, I find comfort in structure, routines, and getting things just right. For a long time, I believed that if I could plan it perfectly, I could control the outcome. But God began to gently show me that what I called "planning" was often my attempt to take control of my life, my family, and even my relationship with Him.

Perfection, I've learned, is often just the illusion of control. When we're wrapped up in controlling everything, we're not truly surrendering. God revealed to me that holding on so tightly was actually keeping me from seeing His hand at work. I wasn't trusting Him with the details. I was attempting to manage Him.

Surrender didn't come easy. I wrestled with it emotionally, spiritually, and practically. It was a process, sometimes painful, often humbling. I've had to come face-to-face with my own limitations, recognize where fear was driving me, and choose surrender over self-sufficiency. Often, I would surrender with my words but still hold on in my heart. There were days when letting go felt like losing my grip on everything safe. But slowly, God showed me that surrender wasn't weakness. It was trust.

Trust didn't mean chaos; it meant being led by Someone who knew the way better than I did.

Maybe you've felt the same way. Maybe you've been striving for excellence, trying to hold everything together as a mom, a wife, or just navigating a busy life. You make the plans, double-check the calendar, and push for perfection, but still feel exhausted and unsure. The more we tighten our grip, the more we realize how little control we really have. It's exhausting to live that way, but there's peace in letting go.

Proverbs 16:9 is a beautiful reminder that while planning has its place, it's the Lord who establishes the path. His steps are steady even when ours feel unsure.

If your plans don't go as expected, it might just be God guiding you to something better.

Letting go doesn't mean giving up. It means giving God room to move. Real freedom comes when we release the need to have it all figured out. Instead of striving for perfection, we can rest in His presence, knowing He has already made a way. Instead of clinging to control, we can trust in His faithfulness. You may set the course, but the Lord is the one who makes it worth walking.

Pray This With Me:

Father, thank You for being patient when I try to take control. Help me to surrender my plans and trust that Your way is always better. Teach me to find peace not in perfection, but in Your presence. In Jesus' name. Amen.

Reflection

Is there a plan you're holding onto too tightly? Ask God today to help you loosen your grip and trust Him with the outcome.

He's In The Fire
By: Shirley Lopez

"He answered and said, 'But I see four men unbound, walking in the midst of the fire, and they are not hurt; and the appearance of the fourth is like a son of the gods.'" (Daniel 3:25, ESV)

There are moments in life that feel like you are walking through fire. It is so hot, so painful, that you're convinced you won't survive. For years, I lived in that fire. Abuse, addiction, betrayal, fear. You name it, I carried it all. Feeling lost, unloved, and invisible, I tried to find relief in all the wrong places. I looked to religious rituals, prayed desperate prayers to saints, and even dabbled in witchcraft, but nothing changed.

Then Jesus found me. I began going to church. I got clean, and for a moment, there was hope. But when my husband relapsed, the abuse returned worse than ever.

One night, the worst I had ever faced, I begged God to help me get out of this situation. I remember whispering to Him saying, *"My babies need me."* The next morning, I made it to church. I met a woman of God and she said something I'll never forget, "You don't have to do this. God's got this." And He did. That day, God provided everything I needed to break free; shelter, protection, and hope.

Like the three men in Daniel 3, the fire didn't consume me. I wasn't alone in the flames. The fourth man, Jesus, was with me in the fire. He was my strength when I had none. He sustained me when I couldn't pray. He defended me when no one else would. He brought me out and delivered me.

Now I know that the God who began a good work in me is faithful to complete it (Philippians 1:6, ESV). The fire that was meant to destroy me, refined me. Now, I live to help others find the same freedom. God restored what the enemy stole. I am now married to a kind and gentle man who loves me, and we serve in ministry together.

If you're in the fire today, hold on. Cry out to Jesus. He hears. He sees. He rescues. When you walk out of the fire, you won't even smell like smoke because He is with you.

Pray This With Me:

Lord, thank You for being with me in the fire. Thank You for not leaving me in my darkest moments. Help me to know that You are near. Surround me with protection, people, and power to walk free. Then use me, Lord, to help bring others out as well. In Jesus' name. Amen.

Reflection:

What fire are you walking through right now? Can you see where Jesus is standing with you in the midst of it?

_____
_____
_____
_____
_____
_____
_____
_____
_____
_____
_____
_____

More Than Enough
By: Lori Bock

"He will renew you and sustain you in your old age."
(Ruth 4:15, NIV)

I've experienced a life marked by profound loss. My childhood was lost to abuse and neglect, my young adulthood in an abusive relationship, broken family connections, and the death of loved ones, sometimes before reconciliation ever came. Many times, I tried to pick up the broken pieces.

Naomi knew this kind of loss too. She lost her husband and both sons in a foreign land, and returned home with her daughter-in-law Ruth, empty and grieving. Even with Ruth by her side, I imagine she felt alone, unseen, and ready to quietly fade away defined by all she had lost.

But the Lord had different plans. He wasn't done with Naomi and He wasn't done with me either.

There came a moment when I had to decide. Would I allow loss and grief to define me, or would I let God fight the battle for me, once and for all? In that divine moment of decision, the Lord asked me to examine where I was, how I got there, and how He could lead me out.

The Lord gently reminded me that He didn't want to be a bystander, He wanted to be the center of my life. I was created for fellowship with Him. He provides in our darkest hour if we surrender it all to Him.

Just as the Lord provided a redeemer through Boaz to Naomi, He reached out His hand to me when my eyes were swollen from crying. He tucked me beneath His feathers and taught me to depend solely on Him. He whispered again and again that something better was ahead and I could trust Him to lead me there.

As women, we feel deeply. The moments when we feel empty and loss are hard. But El Shaddai, the God who is all-sufficient, is with us. We can find everything that we need in Him. Just as He restored Naomi's joy and gave her a new life, He does the same for us.

He is not just enough, He is *more than enough*. I am thankful that Jesus helped me shift my perspective, gave me strength, and filled me with lasting confidence in Him.

Pray This With Me:

Lord, help me fix my eyes on You. You are my Redeemer. Everything I need is found in You. Guide me as I surrender the pain and brokenness. Draw me close to You and remind me I am not alone. You are faithful to restore joy and to sustain me all my days. In Jesus' name. Amen.

Reflection:

Where in your life have you been trying to hold things together on your own? What would it look like to let El Shaddai be your source today?

Woven By Grace
By: Dawn Curiale

"And we know that all things work together for good, for those who love God & are called according to his purpose." (Romans 8:28, NIV)

There are moments when life feels disappointing. A childhood without the fairytale we imagine. Yet Romans 8:28 reminds us that God can transform even broken experiences into a tapestry of hope and redemption.

I grew up without the nurturing care every child deserves. At six, while my parents struggled with drug addiction, I cared for my baby brother, forced to mature quickly. I missed simple joys as a growing teen: a mother's hug, late night lectures, baking together, dressing up for picture day; Dad praying at bedtime; celebrating school events, birthdays, and the milestones of growing up. Baptism, prom, graduation, and college all passed without my mom by my side. She never saw her little girl walk down the aisle or get to meet her granddaughters. Her choices cost her a future. She passed away when I was just 12 years old, shattering my grandparents, who loved her as their only child. I faced another tragic loss when I lost my dad right after our first daughter was born.

In the chaos that was my life, God sent a light. My grandparents took in me and my brother. Their 64-year marriage and steadfast faith became my refuge. They poured unconditional love into my life and took me to church. My grandmother's warmth taught me how to cook and be a wife. My grandfather's tough spirit forged in World War II and having a successful plumbing business taught me resilience. They celebrated every milestone they could, gifting me my first car, a Sweet 16, my dream wedding, and a down payment to build our first home. Their love transformed my painful past into cherished memories, proving that God's grace often arrives in unexpected forms.

At 16, I met a young man who later became my husband. A blessing from God, a protector, provider, unwavering partner, and father. His love is a powerful reminder that even when life isn't perfect, God's plan is at work.

The greatest blessing is now being a mother. I cherish giving my daughters the nurturing care I once longed for. Growing in Jesus with them, celebrating every milestone with love, and fully engaging in their lives. Seeing how God transforms a broken childhood into a story of mercy fills me with gratitude. I can give what I didn't get!

If you're a mother who feels like you've missed it, know it's never too late to be the mom you were meant to be. If you're a grandmother stepping in, never doubt your impact. You are laying a foundation that will shape their lives in ways you may never fully see, but God does. If you are being the best mom you can be, then be thankful and rejoice in His amazing grace.

Pray This With Me:

Lord, in moments of brokenness and loss, thank You for turning my past into a foundation of strength and hope. Help me embrace the present, trusting that You work all things together for good because that's your promise.

Reflection:

Sometimes we forget how powerful thanking someone can be. Think about who God has placed in your life as your source of love and light. How can you express gratitude for their impact?

_____

_____

_____

_____

_____

_____

_____

_____

_____

_____

_____

_____

He Restores My Soul
By: McKenna Prouty

"...He refreshes and restores my soul (life); He leads me in the paths of righteousness for His name's sake." (Psalm 23:3 AMP)

There is so much packed into that short phrase "He restores my soul." It tells of how He, the Good Shepherd, repairs, renews or brings us back to a former state of well-being, particularly the spiritual or innermost part of oneself, and makes us whole again. Life can easily take a toll on our souls, bodies, and minds, as we so often unintentionally carry our pains with us. But He is the Restorer of our souls! We get tired, exhausted from the demands or disappointments in this life, but He says "Come to Me, and I will give you rest." (*Matt 11:28*).

After a series of painful life events, including my own health issues, a newborn who needed medical attention, experiencing attacks of anxiety and fear, and the unexpected and tragic losses of two loved ones which happened just six months apart, my soul had become weary and wounded. Unintentionally, I'd harbored each hurt and disappointment. The Lord was still my Shepherd, and I loved Him and deeply depended on His faithfulness through it all, but I was walking around with wounds I hadn't let Him tend to. I had one hand squeezing tightly onto His but had not let go of the pain clenched in my other hand.

The Great Shepherd is loving and ever so patient. One

day while spending time with the Lord He asked me, "Will you give me your pain and let me heal your heart?" What seemed like an endless amount of tears flowed from my eyes, and I responded, "Yes, Lord, You can have my pain." In my journal, I wrote that I would no longer dwell on my pains or disappointments, but let Him heal the hurts of yesterday. I believed and declared that this was a new chapter and that every pain would serve a great purpose for His glory. From that moment of surrender my soul felt light and free, and He restored my soul and my joy!

Where you've stepped, and where you currently stand is not where you're meant to stay. The disappointments you've experienced are not your destination. The Restorer of your soul is not afraid of your honesty, He welcomes it! Like David, you can pour your heart out before Him. Through your own surrender, partnered with the power of His Holy Spirit, He promises to renew, restore, and make you whole again!

Pray This With Me:

Great Shepherd and Restorer of my soul, thank You for Your tender love and patience towards me. Search my heart and reveal every unaddressed wound I've held on to. Every harbored hurt and injustice done to me, I surrender to You. I thank You, Lord, that You have purposed every experience in my life for my good, and for Your glory! In Jesus' name. Amen.

Reflection:

In Psalm 139:23-24, David prays an honest prayer to the Lord. Take a moment to read these verses, journal, and ask the Lord to search your heart, allowing each pain to bring you back to Him, for He is the Restorer of your soul!

Faith To Believe
By: Shirley Raley

"But without faith it is impossible to please him: for he that cometh to God must believe that he is, and that he is a rewarder of them that diligently seek him." (Hebrews 11:6, KJV)

There was a season in my life when I struggled to hold onto faith. It wasn't sudden. It was subtle. I didn't even recognize it at first. Slowly, through life's challenges, disappointments, and distractions, doubt crept in. While I have walked through many circumstances in my life where my faith was challenged, I have never doubted God. Instead, I would remind myself of Hebrews 11:1, "Faith is the substance of things hoped for, the evidence of things not seen." That kind of faith keeps me focused on Jesus, not on the circumstances.

But one day in prayer, the Lord made it clear: the enemy had been working overtime to weaken my faith. And I realized, that without faith, it's not just hard, it's impossible to please God. Faith is foundational. It is the key that unlocks every promise, every provision, every miracle. If we don't truly believe, we can't fully receive.

Romans 10:17 tells us that "faith comes by hearing, and hearing by the word of God." That means building our faith begins with being in the Word daily. We grow our understanding of who He is by spending time with Him. Over the years, I've learned this in practical ways. Every morning, I set aside time, even if it is just a few minutes, to read Scripture, speak truth over my life, and remember the faithfulness of God.

When I feel weak, I remind myself of Scriptures that stir up faith. Scriptures like:

Fight the good fight of faith and lay hold of eternal life (1 Timothy 6:12).

Having faith the size of a mustard seed can move mountains (Matthew 17:20).

Jesus responds to a mother's faith (Matthew 15:28).

Jesus told a woman she was healed because she believed (Matthew 9:22).

Faith believes that He is. Our Healer, Deliverer, Provider, our Father. Every name of God reveals His nature and His promises. Faith is how we grab hold of them. No matter where you are in your walk with the Lord, whether you are a new Christian or have walked with Jesus for a long time, God rewards those who seek Him with faith. You are not forgotten. He sees you, and He is who He says He is.

Faith isn't always easy, but it is always worth it. So today, choose to believe that He is and that He is a rewarder of those who diligently seek Him.

Pray This With Me:

Father God, increase my faith. Help me grow through Your Word and trust that everything I need whether it is salvation, provision, or healing comes by faith. Reveal more of who You are to me, and help me to apply each of Your names to my life with confidence and trust.

Reflection:

What does your faith say about who God is to you right now? Are there areas where He is inviting you to trust that He is enough?

The Anchor of My Soul
By Valerie Herron

"We have this hope as an anchor for the soul, firm and secure."
(Hebrews 6:19, NIV)

I grew up in the projects, raised by my mother. I didn't know my father. Life was hard. Poverty, struggle, and brokenness were all I knew. Abuse and rejection left wounds that ran deep, and for a long time, I felt lost, like I was drifting with nothing to hold on to.

But in 1985, I met Jesus, and everything changed. He didn't take away my past, but He stepped into it. He took all the hurt, all the pain, and all the emptiness, and He became my anchor. When everything else in my life felt unstable, He held me steady.

Before Christ, I tried to survive on my own, but deep down, I was drowning. I carried shame, fear, and rejection like a heavy weight on my back. But the moment I surrendered my life to Him, He started breaking those chains. His love covered the wounds. His truth silenced the lies I believed. His presence filled the emptiness inside me.

Looking back, I see His hand in every part of my story. When I thought I was alone, He was right there. When I thought I wouldn't make it, He carried me through. When I had no one else to lean on, He was my firm foundation.

I won't pretend life has been easy since then. Storms still come, struggles still rise, but the difference is I'm not drifting anymore. I know who holds me. I know who I belong to. The same God who kept me through my past is the same God keeping me now. The Great I Am has been my everything. He is my rescuer, my safe place, my unshakable foundation. Through every trial, every season, and every storm, He has never let me go.

Now, think about your own story. Can you remember a time when God showed up and became the anchor of your soul? Maybe it was in a moment of deep pain, a season of uncertainty, or a time when you felt like you had nothing left. Take a minute to reflect on His goodness and how He met you right where you were, how He rescued you, and how He provided when you didn't see a way out. Let that truth sink in. Take a moment to tell Him what He means to you, then pause to hear what He says You mean to Him.

Pray This With Me:

Lord, thank You for being my anchor. When life felt like too much, You held me together. Thank You for turning my pain into a testimony and reminding me that I'm never alone. Help me to trust You more, knowing You are always faithful. In Jesus' name. Amen.

Reflection:

What storms has God carried you through? Take a moment to think about how He has been your anchor and thank Him for His faithfulness. If you're facing a storm now, will you trust Him to hold you steady?

Living With Purpose
By: Jenna Norris

"Many are the plans in a person's heart, but it is the Lord's purpose that prevails." (Proverbs 19:21, NIV)

When I was in high school, my extracurricular activities included football, basketball, and wrestling. I was not a participant, but I was there as a junior athletic trainer, and I loved it. It involved people, cheering them on, and helping in various ways. My plan after graduation was to pursue a career in sports medicine.

That was my plan. But God had another.

Not long after graduation, I attended a series of services at a summer camp. I had friends attending and my pastor was preaching. I'd always known God had a plan for my life, and I was determined to hear His voice loud and clear. I came expecting every night and of course, it was the last night when He spoke, or maybe I was just finally listening. I don't remember the message. I just remember standing in the back with tears streaming down my face, waiting for the altar call. The moment it opened, I made a beeline to the front. All I could say was, "Yes, Lord."

From that yes, I spent a few months as a missionary, went to Bible school, got married, entered full-time ministry, and have never looked back.

"Yes" to His plan. His purpose. His will. Yes to the hard times, the stretching, the tears, the victories, and the refining fire. Yes to trust Him with every detail. Yes, even when I don't understand. Yes even though I can't see what's ahead. Yes even when life gets hard. Yes because there's nothing to go back to. I've burned the ships and surrendered my plan. Yes!

And it's that yes that continually pushes me forward into the purpose He has for my life.

I have found more fulfillment in saying yes to Jesus than anything else this world has to offer. His plan is perfect. He is trustworthy, even if it looks different from my own plan.

When life gets hard, and trust me, it does, I choose to refresh my yes to Jesus. His plans are always better than my own. Saying yes isn't always glamorous or loud, sometimes it's quiet and looks like choosing to show up, do the hard thing, and stay the course.

And every time you do that, you're saying, "Jesus, I'm still yours. I still believe. I still want what You want."

Today, I want to encourage you to refresh your own yes to Jesus. Yes to His perfect will. Yes to the adventure. Yes to the unknown. Yes to the growth. Yes to the tears and the triumphs. Yes! Not for your sake, but for the sake of those you're called to impact, influence, and serve.

Pray This With Me:

Jesus, today I refresh my yes to You. I choose to step into Your purpose for my life even when I can't see the full picture. Strengthen my heart, renew my trust, and help me to stay faithful. I surrender my plans to Yours. Let my life be a reflection of a steady and surrendered heart. In Jesus' name. Amen.

Reflection:

Where do you need to refresh your yes today?

God Can Use Anyone
By: Amber Lopez

"...People judge by outward appearance, but the Lord looks at the heart." (1 Samuel 16:7, NLT)

This year I embarked on a new journey teaching middle school English and Bible. If you know anything about being a teacher, you know the teacher learns right along with the students. This has been the case in my 7th grade Bible class. We have been on a journey through the Old Testament following the lineage of Jesus in the lives of unsuspecting characters.

As we began our study with Adam and Eve, Noah, Abraham, and Jacob, we began to notice a theme: God can use anyone. God spoke this to us as a whole class one day as we were reading and studying, and it has become a concept we remind ourselves of almost daily. None of these characters deserved to be the carrier of the seed of the Messiah. They didn't fit the mold of what would be expected to carry the lineage of the Great I Am. But God doesn't judge us based on what we look like on the outside. He doesn't judge us by what position we hold, what our title is, or even our past mistakes. He sees a vessel that He can use to accomplish His plans.

Abraham was called out of idolatry to be the father of a nation and a blessing to the whole world (Genesis 12:1-3).

Joseph was the youngest son, sold into slavery, and

spent years in prison before he saw God's plan for good over his life (Genesis 45:5).

Moses was adopted by the enemy, a murderer, and scared to take the leadership position God called Him to, yet God used Him to rescue His people from slavery (Exodus 3:10).

David was the youngest son, overlooked even by his father, an adulterer, and a murderer whose descendants would produce the Seed that would redeem the world (2 Samuel 7:16).

These are just a few examples of people God used who didn't fit the mold. You are also an example of the concept that God can use anyone. We all are. God can use you when you feel unworthy and when you make mistakes. He even uses our mistakes for our good and His glory.

God's reminder to Samuel the prophet in 1 Samuel 16 is the same reminder He gives us today. He doesn't judge you, choose you, or call you based off of your outward circumstances. He chooses you, calls you, and uses you based on your heart.

Pray This With Me:

God, I turn my heart toward You today. Remind me that I am worthy, important, and useful even when I feel like I'm not. I believe that You can use me no matter what circumstances are going on around me. Help my heart to become open and ready to do Your will.

Reflection:

As you read through the Bible, take note of where He uses the unexpected person to fulfill His will.

It has truly been an honor to walk this 21-day journey with you. Through these pages, you've been given a glimpse into the hearts and lives of women who have encountered Jesus through moments of hardship and triumph, in seasons of questions and doubt, yet choosing to worship through the trials, and celebrating His goodness through it all.

This may be the final page of this book, but God is not finished writing your story. Our prayer is that you have been encouraged, strengthened, and challenged and that your walk with the Lord has deepened along the way.

Whatever season you may find yourself in, remember that Jesus is with you and that He is and always will be

Forever Faithful.

Women of Grace is a ministry of:

Grace World Outreach Church
20366 Cortez Blvd
Brooksville, FL 34609

www.graceworldag.org

Made in the USA
Columbia, SC
19 April 2025